D1541167

Planted with a Purpose

ALSO BY T. D. JAKES

Planted with a Purpose

God Turns Pressure into Power

T. D. JAKES

New York   Nashville

FaithWords
Hachette Book Group
1290 Avenue of the Americas, New York, NY 10104
faithwords.com
twitter.com/faithwords

First edition: April 2020

FaithWords is a division of Hachette Book Group, Inc. The FaithWords name and logo are trademarks of Hachette Book Group, Inc.

The publisher is not responsible for websites (or their content) that are not owned by the publisher.

The Hachette Speakers Bureau provides a wide range of authors for speaking events. To find out more, go to www.hachettespeakersbureau.com or call (866) 376-6591.

Unless otherwise noted, Scripture quotations are taken from the Holy Bible, New International Version®, NIV®. Copyright ©1973, 1978, 1984, 2011 by Biblica, Inc.™ Used by permission of Zondervan. All rights reserved worldwide. www.zondervan.com. The "NIV" and "New International Version" are trademarks registered in the United States Patent and Trademark Office by Biblica, Inc.™

Scriptures marked (AMP) are taken from the Amplified® Bible (AMP), copyright © 2015 by The Lockman Foundation. Used by permission. www.Lockman.org

Scripture quotations marked ESV are taken from the ESV® Bible (The Holy Bible, English Standard Version®), copyright © 2001 by Crossway, a publishing ministry of Good News Publishers. Used by permission. All rights reserved.

Scriptures marked (AMPC) are from the Amplified® Bible (AMPC), copyright © 1954, 1958, 1962, 1964, 1965, 1987 by The Lockman Foundation. Used by permission. www.Lockman.org

Library of Congress Control Number: 2019957152

ISBNs: 978-1-5460-1781-3 (hardcover); 978-1-5460-1782-0 (ebook)

Printed in the United States of America

LSC-C

10 9 8 7 6 5 4 3 2

Contents

CHAPTER 1

When You Are Crushed

Crushed. Broken. Lost. Hopeless.

When the floor beneath you opens up and swallows you into a free fall, you find yourself suddenly submerged in a flood of emotions, thoughts, and questions. In the midst of unexpected pain or inevitable loss, pitiful thoughts assail you as you sink into the emotional quicksand of life's messy places, the muddy pits where everything you once held dear and true is questioned, dissected, and shaken to the core.

Here, your safety zone and all presumed constants are revealed to be far more fragile than you had ever realized. This is where you wonder if you will ever be on your feet again, and if so, then how you will summon the strength to move on. This is where your faith is tested, where it's refined and purified. But such knowledge is little comfort in the midst of the blazing wildfires of life engulfing all you thought you knew and reducing expectations to ashes. Like a deer trying to follow a familiar wooded path in the midst of a forest fire, you begin running in circles, facing dead ends and disturbing detours, uncertain which way to go. Choking on collateral smoke, you're left weary and wasted, calloused and confused, depleted and discouraged, frightened and frozen in place.

Part of the confusion results from the way life's greatest successes often bleed into the blur of your most painful moments. Because even in the moments of your greatest anguish, you often find unexpected blessings alongside and commingled with your losses.

One of the biggest losses I've ever suffered was the death of my mother. But even as I watched my beloved mother waste away—a part of my crushing—I marveled at the way God continued to bless my ministry, my businesses, and my platform of influence. Leaders from around the globe began inviting me to visit, speak, and preach in venues I had once dreamed about seeing. My books were becoming best sellers, and movie producers were interested in taking *Woman, Thou Art Loosed!* to the big screen as a feature film. I would have traded all of it to restore my mother's mind, body, and spirit, but God had a purpose.

And when my daughter was pregnant at thirteen— again what I thought was a part of the crushing period. Critics and haters of me and my ministry would pounce on such news like piranhas. Even as Sarah's health and well-being and the life of my grandchild growing within her remained my priority, I knew I would be foolish to ignore others' public responses to our family's private situation. The irony, of course, was that the one person I would usually have turned to for comfort, wise counsel, and encouragement was no longer with me. I would never have my mother back.

I can't tell you the number of nights I cried silently, staring out the windows of my home into the darkness. I never imagined studying the windowpanes would become my default hobby following my mother's death. But night after night, there I was again, gazing into a dark night that reflected the one in my own soul.

I am not one to wallow in self-pity, but when I experienced that one-two punch to my soul, I could only sink into the quicksand of my sadness. So many nights I stared out the windows of my home, seeing in the darkness nothing but the reflection of my own glistening tears as they coursed down my face. I usually prefer to take constructive action in the midst of any mistake, mishap, or misadventure, but my new reality left me drained of my determination.

Nighttime holds a special place for our more desperate tears. We wrestle with trying to find sleep but are kept awake by the thoughts of our problems, the rehashing of our circumstances. The silence all around us somehow makes our thoughts louder and our situations direr.

Such was my season at that time. I felt trapped in my pain. Leveled by circumstances beyond my control. Powerless to protect those I loved the most. Unable to enjoy my life's many blessings.

Crushed.

I believe that it is in these difficult moments—the crushing time—that it is even more crucial that we begin seeing that the plans we have imagined for our lives cannot compare to God's strategy for fulfilling our divine purpose. Once accepted and acted upon, this line of thinking causes a massive shift in our perceptions, decisions, and behavior. We finally realize that we have been thinking on too small a level in contrast to a God whose endgame for our destinies focuses on eternity instead of something temporary. We sprint to win the race we perceive we're running, but instead God is training us for the Master's marathon!

Detours of Life

I've noticed again and again that routes to progress and success often take detours. Never is there a straight path toward either of them. Our advancement inevitably includes out-of-the-way breakdowns and unplanned pit stops that seemingly have nothing to do with our plans and purpose. We steadily travel down life's highway toward our future until we find ourselves taking an exit to a place that wasn't even on our map. It's an unscheduled stop and perceived pause in our progress that threatens to destroy everything we have accomplished thus far.

Stranded and sidelined, we begin feeling anxious, afraid, and uncertain. As if striking out into something new wasn't jarring enough, we become anxious because we didn't plan on making any stops, let alone in deserted places. But then we discover something there that compels us, inspires us, and motivates us in a new direction. Suddenly we begin blazing a new trail that leads us toward a satisfaction and fulfillment that exceeds anything we could have found using our original itinerary.

And it's all because we got lost along the way to where we thought we were going. Only God knew we weren't lost any more than the people of Israel wandering in the desert for forty years before entering the Promised Land were lost. You see, I'm convinced life's devastating detours often become the miraculous milestones charting a new path toward God's future for us. The tumultuous trying, testing, and crushing we experience in those places is necessary for our advancement. More important, it's imperative that our life's painful detours be hidden from us before they occur, lest we forfeit the entire trip toward our future because of our discomfort with being diverted. In the moment, these crushing places feel like they will destroy us and derail our journey from what we've determined is our destination. We question whether the suffering we're encountering will be the end of all we've accomplished and pursued thus far. We wonder where God is and why He would allow us to hurt so deeply.

But these crushing places also reveal there's more to our lives than what we had planned. They force us to reset our compass on our Creator. As we look for His guidance and follow His direction, the crushing becomes the creation of something new.

Consider the way tons of rock and soil crush carbon deposits into diamonds. From the carbon's perspective, the weight of the world literally destroys you—but it also creates something new, something rare and beautiful. Crushing places reveal that there is more to our lives than we had planned. The truly invaluable, marvelous, and eternal aspects of our identity and ultimate destiny are displayed to us there.

It is specifically upon the areas of personal crushing that I want us to focus our exploration in these pages. We don't need to linger on what the moments of crushing actually feel like, because every person of destiny has or will become familiar with pain. The question that needs to be answered during our crushing is whether or not the suffering we are encountering is the end of all we have accomplished. To that inquiry, I sincerely and wholeheartedly believe the answer is a resounding "No!"

You might feel resigned to a life that's less than God's best for you because you cannot allow yourself to imagine that the best is yet to come. Even though the event itself may have been years or decades ago, the trauma of your tragedy may continue to trap you in the past moment, leaving you to focus on the broken stems and crushed fruit of your past achievements rather than the possibility of maximizing your potential through our Father's divine process. Regardless of where you are, we all wrestle with the unexpected impact that crushing leaves on our souls.

You have probably asked some of these questions, but I want to encourage you to dig deep and think about them now as we move forward with exploring how this season can point directly toward your purpose, the one you are being planted and groomed and nourished for right now. As you journey with me through this book, ask yourself:

Could there be sanctity in my suffering?

Could my worst moments truly become more than shameful secrets of my past mistakes?

What if I could see my life as God sees it?

What if my best moments are waiting ahead?

My friend, I'm convinced God can use the weight crushing your soul right now to create His choicest product—if you will let Him.

Crushing is not the end!

Reflect on how you felt during a time of crushing. What questions did you ask? What emotions did you feel?

CHAPTER 2

The Wait

Anyone who knows me knows that I absolutely love to cook. Whenever I have leisure time I head to the kitchen, and I have a few rules. One is that I don't like to follow recipes, savoring instead the culinary creativity that must motivate master chefs. My other requisite is a group of family and friends to indulge my endeavors—and they must be hungry! A few polite bites are an insult. I love to cook for people who loosen their belts when they're eating, and consider their grunts and lack of choice manners to be the greatest compliments—along with asking for seconds and thirds, of course.

My passion for cooking meals for loved ones originated when I was growing up. Because our family didn't have much materially, my siblings and I didn't get excited about gifts at Christmas and birthdays—but we were exuberant in anticipation of the food! I remember my mother preparing and cooking food for days before Christmas. You could smell the aromas wafting throughout the house, and if you were lucky, she would allow you to lick the spoon and taste a little bit beforehand. As a result, my wife and I now delight in showing the same love my mother put into the preparation of special meals for the celebrations we enjoy.

From all those years of watching my mother prepare food for the family, and from my own limited experience in the kitchen, I've realized an important lesson: *quality takes time.*

While most people tend to agree with me, no one particularly enjoys waiting patiently for the turkey to come out of the oven or for the pie crust to be made from scratch. We want the quality, but we don't want to wait for it.

The amount of work it takes to produce a great meal

reminds me of the way we discover and utilize what God has placed inside us: the core gifts, talents, abilities, and preferences unique to our Creator's design. Throughout our lives and amid the diverse variables of our particular environments, the same God who placed those seeds and gifts within us seeks to cultivate and harvest His initial investment in order to multiply it even more. Our Maker wishes to see these internal seeds and latent talents grow, mature, and bring forth abundant fruit used for something more.

Because God is the originator of everything in us, and because we are created in His image, it makes sense that He desires to see His creativity exercised in His creations. If the cycle of nature calls for us to reproduce after our own kind, we logically see that same inclination in the Creator, who set this cycle into motion. His intention is for the seeds placed inside us to grow, develop, mature, and maximize our growth. Our current world, however, demands hurriedly produced results, and many of us have despised the day of small beginnings found in seeds. It is a fact that seeds take time to grow. You do not plant a seed today and expect a harvest tomorrow. We often don't exercise the patience to wait and watch and wait some more. But patience may be the ultimate source of quality control for what God is simmering in your soul and cooking up in your life. The real mystery of God is hidden in the beauty of the seed and revealed in His wonderful use of the growth process.

So if we abort the development process, we are compromising the power of the promise God has placed within us. After all, the process of a seed becoming what is promised is the underlying realization of our destiny.

Biological Signs

God is so good that He gives us signs to remind us of this very process as we strive to grow into our purpose.

Consider the biological growth of a human being from conception to full maturity. The sperm, or seed, of an adult male fertilizes and fuses with the ovum, or egg, of an adult female. That fertilized egg develops into an embryo and then a fetus over a nine-month period. At the end of the fetal stage, a baby is born into the world. Over a period of years, the infant grows into a toddler and then advances into childhood, adolescence, and finally adulthood. Notwithstanding any illnesses or other challenges, not a single child brought into this world ever remains in seed form. Not one of us is a large, fertilized ovum roaming the neighborhood. Each of us became something greater. We grew into the full maturity of our potential.

Just as He intended with Christ, God never destined us to remain in seed form. He did not design us in such a fashion because nothing eternal could ever exist temporarily. God's desire has always been to reconnect us back to Himself and take us from finite to infinite. One of the things I love most about God's Word is how God addresses every season of life: beginning, middle, and end.

If Jesus is God's only begotten Son, how could we not assign the same timeless and eternal nature to Him that we view in God? In fact, this truth is the foundation from which John begins his gospel account of the life of Christ: "In the beginning

was the Word, and the Word was with God, and the
Word was God. He was with God in the beginning.
Through Him all things were made; without Him
nothing was made that has been made. In Him was
life, and that life was the light of all mankind. The
light shines in the darkness, and the darkness has not
overcome it.... The Word became flesh and made His
dwelling among us. We have seen His glory, the glory
of the one and only Son, who came from the Father,
full of grace and truth" (John 1:1–5, 14).

Since Jesus is the very fruition of God's Word, He
must be the beginning, or seed, of our lives as well.
The seed, then, was already present because Jesus is
simultaneously the vine and seed. Therefore, the seed
and vine are one.

Confused? I know it's mind-bending and requires
some reflection. Perhaps the apostle Paul explained it
best in his letter to the Galatians: "The promises were
spoken to Abraham and to his seed. Scripture does
not say 'and to seeds,' meaning many people, but 'and
to your seed,' meaning one person, who is Christ"
(Gal. 3:16).

With Jesus being the seed promised to Abraham

as an inheritance, we must ask ourselves what the promise was inside of Jesus that was to be fulfilled. The promise carried by Christ is a bountiful harvest of fruit. Since Jesus is both seed and vine, we are the promised fruit-bearing branches that spring forth from Him. During the Last Supper, we see the Seed of Abraham speaking with his spiritual offspring, who would soon take up the task of not only bearing fruit but also pointing other dormant seeds of promise back to the life-giving Savior, Jesus Christ. If Jesus is the seed that grew into a vine that produced us as fruit-bearing branches, the fruit we produce and the lives we live are seeds that God intends for a greater purpose.

The Process of Making Wine

Think about the winemaking process. The winemaking process is an analogy that permeates the Bible in both the Old and New Testaments. Addressing an agrarian culture, many of the images, metaphors, and parables of Scripture focus on planting, tending, gardening, and harvesting. The journey from seed to sapling, from grape to greatness, consistently reminds us of the process. These symbols lend themselves to our spiritual growth and development as well.

When we first step into an area where we are able to grow, is that not analogous to us being planted? Later, when we encounter a blessing in our lives, can it not be seen as fruit to be enjoyed? When our family and friends revel in our success, is that not akin to those farmers of old relishing the harvest? When our harvest doesn't go as planned, however, and our fruitful blessing is stripped from us and carelessly trampled, does that not strongly resemble the winepress, the device used to crush grapes and drain their juice for winemaking?

Of course, all of this depends on your point of view. If you were a winemaker, or vintner, as they're often called, you would be all too familiar with each step in the process of making wine. However, if you were the grapevine, the removal of your fruit and its destruction under the feet of those who seem not to care would give you a completely different perspective.

In the midst of our painful crushing, we realize

that the blessing found in the production of fruit in our lives was never God's end goal. Our latest crop of fruit was merely part of an ongoing, greater process. The Master Vintner knows there's something much more worthwhile beyond the production of fruit—the potency of its juice fermented into wine. To the vine, however, the fruit seems to be everything, season after season, storm after storm, sun and rain, spring and fall. But what if you shifted your paradigm to wine-making instead of fruit growing? Could it be possible that your current predicament is the winepress God uses to transform your grapes into His wine? Could being crushed be a necessary part of the process to fulfill God's plan for your life? Could you be on the verge of victory despite walking through the valley of broken vines?

We were created to be more than temporary fruit— *We are His eternal wine in the making!*

But, as you already know, this beautiful winemaking process is not easy and not without work. In fact, I believe the process of fermentation into eternal wine happens over time and in dirty places.

What we see in the natural realm is a reflection of

what we see spiritually because both are intertwined with one another. As a result, we encounter another version of natural child-into-adult development in our spiritual nature. In the spiritual realm, there is a process we enter into in which God cultivates and develops us into a healthy vine in His vineyard, and God has made Jesus to be the type of vine we are to exemplify in each stage of life. Jesus is our perfect example, our model of this intended maturation.

For instance, we already know Christ to be the Seed of Abraham. He came in our likeness so that He would be familiar with each of our trials, difficulties, and temptations (Heb. 4:15–16). In essence, He experienced all of the growth pains we would experience. As Jesus grew in stature, we know that He grew in favor with God and with men and began bearing fruit (Luke 2:52). Though He was an adult producing a wonderful harvest during His three years of ministry, Jesus was not meant to simply work miracle after miracle. His life on earth was intended to move from something temporary to something eternal.

Though Christ became a physical adult, His spirit carried the even greater promise of an eternal harvest—and not just one made up of miracles that would be temporarily praised. In order for that spiritual promise to be birthed, the supernatural seed had to enter into its own version of development. Like any seed that would sprout, it had to be planted. In essence, everything the seed knows about itself has to end. The seed, then, must die just as Christ died so that He could give birth to us as God's spiritual children, His divine offspring.

If we are called to be like Christ, to become like Him as we are called by God (1 Cor. 11:1), we must accept the fact that we will experience a similar growth process. As we undergo maturation, we come to understand that our temporary fruit was never the endgame of an everlasting Master, but rather just a single step in the process of making eternal wine. As a result, our spiritual development from seeds to mature fruit-bearing branches demands that we confront a step that many of us grapple with understanding: growing in dirty places.

When everything falls apart in our lives, we are broken but not destroyed. The exterior husk we've all relied on for so long begins to fail us as the waters of life soften our protective coating. The tender inner life and identity of who we are is naked and helpless in front of those things that threaten the only existence we know. When we are placed in perilous circumstances, we rush to secure ourselves and hold everything in place. We shoot roots into the soil beneath us in hope of anchoring ourselves against life's storms. We yearn for someone or something to hold us, lift us, and sustain us, but too often we droop and wilt in the winds of our isolation and loneliness.

But what if God is doing something amazing in the midst of those dirty places? What if we are being presented with an opportunity to grow, to become what we are purposed and designed to become?

Knowing that your dirty places could be the very place you will gain what is needed for your next phase of life, how will you respond to them differently?

CHAPTER 3

The Burial

While we are in the midst of our crushing periods, we don't often stop and think about the process. Most of us just want it to end; we want to find the solution and move forward. We enjoy knowing we are gifted and have the ability to do something great, yet we don't smile brightly when we are placed in the refining process. But I challenge you—even in the midst of your crushing—to fully consider the seed and the process used to grow it from a small kernel to a plant.

What happens to a seed if it's not planted? Jesus said, "Very truly I tell you, unless a kernel of wheat falls to the ground and dies, it remains only a single seed. But if it dies, it produces many seeds" (John 12:24).

We cannot rightfully ask our Vinedresser to skip out on the development of our lives simply because we are uncomfortable with being alone in dark places. To keep a seed from being planted is to condemn that seed to never realizing its full potential. It is a fact that seeds are meant to be covered and die.

No matter who we are, where we are in life, or where we've come from, we must begin to appreciate the ugly stages of our inception. When we allow the Lord to shift our mindset, we begin to see that everything that has ever happened to us has happened for a reason. If we look back at the sprout that pushed itself through the ceiling of dirt above it, we discover reasons behind our adversity that were previously invisible and unimaginable. Now they are suddenly apparent and miraculous when we arrive at the fruit-bearing stage.

Looking back at different periods of my life, I remember how fearful I was. Now, standing upon just over forty years of ministry, I look at those places and realize they were integral to where God has taken me and where He will continue to take me. I see that each growth interval of my life was preceded by a planting phase where I was buried in a dirty place. I began to understand that the stages in my life where, at the time, I was certain I was about to meet my end were seed stages for the next season. I could not have produced the fruit without the frustration. And God could not ferment my fruit into His wine for maximum potency without my willingness to relinquish it to His winepress.

Though I have not liked the process, my faith has grown deeper as I discovered this new viewpoint. I have been changed by this shift in perspective as I accept that God never intended to lead me to a dead place and leave me there. The seeming death through which He escorted me was merely the precipice of a new beginning, and a new beginning is what the planting and death of each seed is all about. Through those stages, I arrived at the truth: *God wasn't burying me—He was planting me.*

Transformation requires sacrifice, and I wonder if you have misinterpreted the Vinedresser's intention.

Instead of condemning you to a graveyard, which is what you may feel, God is planting you in richer soil for greater fruit.

Remember, God is at work, and there's no place too dirty for Him to use as the rich soil of your maturation and spiritual fruition. Wherever you are, or whatever your dirty place might be, look around you and allow the Master to adjust your thinking. After all, God is not done with you yet. Quality takes time, and you are God's masterpiece.

God's Strategy

Have you noticed our human propensity to brood over the disastrous at the expense of the prosperous? We do anything and everything to avoid the hideous experiences of life, never grasping the fact that the sprouted seedling could never understand the process of cultivation from its own limited point of view. Similarly, it is a striking blow to our limited comprehension of God to accept that He would use the most unorthodox procedures and inhospitable environments to develop us into something more, something teeming with the potential for dynamic growth. But what's better than being undone and marred in the hands of the Master if a new way of living and abundance are the promised results? What if all you've suffered in your life without was necessary to cultivate your greatness within?

We fight against God's sovereignty because we dislike where His process has placed us. Where the Lord found you, however, and where He decides to plant you can be quite different. We're all being grafted into a supernaturally cultivated vine, and this merging takes time and costs us the comfort of everything we consider comfortable and familiar. Having your life upended and every recognizable detail removed from your environment produces trauma.

But the Master is intentional in how He relocates the wild shoots of our lives and moves them into the unrecognizable fields of promise. This is the secret to accepting the visible violence of turbulent times: we must remember that soil must be upturned or else it will go fallow, depleted of its nutrients and minerals and unable to accommodate new growth.

The act of cultivation is married to our purposeful displacement, because anything grown in the wild does so without the careful hand and watchful eye of an intentional vinedresser. Cultivation speaks order into chaos, orchestrates harmony from disharmony, draws care from carelessness, and provides direction to aimlessness. Cultivation wants to grow and create where growth and creation seem to be impossible.

Any farmer or agriculturist understands this, but many of us miss the point within our own lives. We choose our own way of seeing, believing, and acting because we think we know better. As a result, we miss our true identity and the blessings we could have had if we would have simply submitted to the process.

God is adamantly invested in developing us into something we would never be without His direct intervention. When we find ourselves broken, battered, beaten, and bruised by our circumstances, it's possible that the Master who we're praying will remove and solve the problem is the very One who sanctioned it and is using it to accomplish some greater effect.

Out of all my years of teaching, preaching,

mentoring, and living through hellish ordeals, I believe that our maturation requires that we be constricted to His methods and imprisoned by His purpose. You see, I've had the privilege of meeting some of the most interesting people in the world—and no one was more surprised than I was! In my wildest dreams, I never imagined sitting across from the CEO of AT&T or getting to see Oprah Winfrey move and operate in the worlds of film, television, and print media, because the seed of who I was could not comprehend the fruit I would bear and the wine I would become.

I didn't suddenly wake up as the person you see today. I was developed into this, and God is still fostering even more within me. None of what you see in my life today happened because of magic, luck, or happenstance. All of it is the fruit of purpose, cultivation, and time, the culmination of myriad random details coalescing into something beautiful. And I believe God is doing the same in you, through His own purposeful strategies.

To put it simply, the seed doesn't understand the vine that it's becoming. Everything that occurs in its life appears to be happenstance because all it can see is the muck and mire that it's trying to escape. It's when we are vines that we can look back at what we used to be and notice that what appeared to be accidents, incidents, and coincidence converged to produce what we are and the fruit that hangs from our branches.

Will you let Him work, or will you run from the challenging seasons? I promise you what's on the other side of your growth is much better than you can imagine.

God doesn't expect you to wrap your mind around how you should grow. He only expects your trust as you seemingly stumble your way through the process, because growth is riddled with constant change and correction. It's through the stumbling in our lives that the Master takes us from the seed stages to the fruit-bearing stages. And it's through our own planning, stubbornness, and need to have our way that we derail ourselves. But God did not arrange every single step of your life to this point to leave the weight of your future solely in your own hands. He has not brought you this far to culminate in a cul-de-sac of constraint. To the human eye, He provides a random blessing or lesson, but it's all part of your cultivation. With God, nothing is wasted. He redeems even our darkest moments by allowing us to become a prism of His light.

Now that you've considered the trials it takes for a seed to become a plant, use your own plant to reflect on the process. As you care for it, water it, and await its growth, remember that your life is a part of this maturation. Wherever you are in the planting process, trust God to develop His purpose in your life. You have been planted with a purpose.

CHAPTER 4

When Trouble Comes

Take heed: if your life is suddenly unstable and you notice an increase in the amount of mess and manure placed upon you, pay close attention. It is a sign from the Lord for you to look carefully for the areas where your growth might have stalled. The vinedresser applies an extra amount of dung to a plant that stubbornly refuses to grow, because the messes of life serve as the vitamins required for healthy fruit. The irony, of course, is that what we abhor is simultaneously what we need the most. It's the Master's expert use of trials, tribulations, and trouble to stimulate us that force us to produce the best grapes for making wine.

Most of us underestimate all that the Master has invested in us. The time, the location, the planting, and even the suffering serve His singular purpose. If the Vinedresser would go to such lengths to grow us and help us produce fruit, why do we think we are unable to handle the trouble He allows to come our way? Why do we believe that any instance of hardship and pain in our lives is the end? If He is omnipotent, omnipresent, and omniscient—and He is—then we have to accept that He has constructed us with full knowledge of the obstacles in our paths.

Nevertheless, when trouble comes, we so often ignore His perfect plan and entertain the doubting questions of the enemy. We allow our inner critics to become bullhorns of belittling comments and biting critiques of our relationship with God, doubting that He loves us and wants what is best for us. In fact, our spiritual enemy loves to undermine our faith in God by questions such as these:

*How could God know what He's doing if you're still
sick?*

*You've been living check-to-check all your life, trying
to get ahead. How could there be divine wisdom
in that?*

*If God knows everything and is all-powerful,
then He could have stopped the cancer from
spreading. Do you really think He knows what He's
doing?*

*Why would God let you lose your job after all you've
done for that place? What good can possibly come
from being unemployed?*

*How could God allow that relationship to end? If
He loved you, would He really want you to be by
yourself?*

If you've ever had thoughts like these, you are not
alone. I, too, have been lost in the mental maze of
such miserable meditations. These questions haunt
us all in the midst of the labyrinth of laments. We
wallow in doubt and worry and allow ourselves to be
consumed by fear and anxiety. Our complaints and

doubts, however, come from an individual who has forgotten that God has specifically tailored our struggles so that we would produce succulent fruit.

The thought that we've been chosen for the pain confuses us because we believe that God is stumbling into our future just like we are. We assume that He's unaware of what's around the corners of life, that His point of view is as limited as our own. We don't immediately warm up to a God who would say, "Ah! Now, this broken home is the perfect spot for him to become an excellent father!" For what loving God would put the object of His love through such trauma? It's when we're planted in pain and pressed by His purpose that we shake our fists and demand that He immediately cease His plan and assist with ours.

We waste valuable time and energy anytime we think we know better than God—even when we can't make sense of the circumstances in which we feel buried. *Especially* when we cannot see anything except darkness and can only smell the stench of decay. During such moments, we must trust that something is growing. Something is being birthed in the invisible realities we likely cannot see. How do I know this? Because the Lord has made it clear: "'For I know the plans I have for you,' declares the LORD, 'plans to prosper you and not to harm you, plans to give you hope and a future'" (Jer. 29:11).

Displacement

The time when trouble comes, when you are displaced and disoriented, is no fun. No one wants to go through it. You're tired and feel you're almost at your end. You've been displaced and uprooted from everything familiar in your life, and you're looking for anything to help you stabilize yourself against the uncertainty of tomorrow. However, I believe it is at this time, at this season, that you should stop looking for exterior assistance and allow God to develop and stimulate the dormant muscles of your core. This is the season when your endurance, resolve, and fortitude are enhanced. Though you've done everything you can to get the Master's attention in hopes that He would relent from His plan to crush you, I assure you that He is not out to destroy you. On the contrary, He's out to remake you, remodel you, and renew you. And He has given His word that your momentary discomfort will bring about the most profitable end.

The Father hasn't transplanted you and invested all the time and energy into growing you only to turn around and abandon you. He has placed you in the field that is uniquely equipped with the sunlight, rain, and even the dung you need to become a vine capable of bearing fruit. This field isn't your cemetery. It's the controlled environment the Master is using to cultivate you.

If we truly see Christ as the first fruits of something new and wonderful in the earth, then are we willing to follow His example? Do we really perceive Him as the vine from which we spring and have life? If we, the branches, are reconnected back to the Father, who is the Husbandman, through Christ, our True Vine, in such a way that we now bear His image, it makes sense that we would undergo the same maturation process. If we follow that line of thought, we must be planted in life's dirty places, because Jesus was planted as a seed—by coming to our world in human form—with the intent that He would rise and give new life to everyone who is birthed from Him. In order for us to be born again, Jesus had to be planted and die before resurrecting to new life.

Unfortunately, we aren't allowed the luxury of having clarified hindsight of the ordeals that befall us until they have passed. We have to trust that the Husbandman knows what He is doing. While accepting that my daughter was pregnant and my mother was gone, I still had a litany of questions that I asked the Father. He remained silent for a while, and that caused me to seek Him even more. I had to walk by faith and not by sight, which is what He asks of all of us.

Please understand that it is from the depths of dark and dirty places in our lives that we scream for God's attention and help while misunderstanding that, just like with a natural seed, it is the microbes in the soil of life that eat away at our efforts to protect ourselves from harm. Right when you've lost all hope, you see something you have never witnessed before.

When you resolve within yourself that maybe, just maybe, where you are is your assigned lot in life, God remains vocally silent but reminds you of His promise by showing you the light you have never seen. Breaking through the filthy soil of where you were placed in life, you sprout and rise to continue seeing another world of possibilities and say the famous words of David: "It is good for me that I have been afflicted, that I might learn Your statutes" (Ps. 119:71 AMPC).

An unplanted seed is nothing more than constrained potential. We love the thought of being gifted and having the ability to do something great, but we don't smile so brightly when we are placed in the refining processes of life. But aren't these two intimately connected? How can we have one without the other? We cannot rightfully ask the Master Husbandman to skip out on the development of our lives simply because we are uncomfortable with being alone in dark places.

Everything that has ever happened to you happened for a reason. If we look back at the sprout that pushed itself through the ceiling of dirt above it, we arrive at the conclusion that we will understand the reasons behind our adversity when we arrive at the fruit-bearing stage. For when does a pot know exactly what its purpose is? Is it not when the potter is done forming and molding it?

Those areas and times in which the death of a dream, an assignment, or vision seems to stalk your every move are nothing more than entrances into the next realm of your life. Do not run from them. Embrace them, because the proverbial death of what you are trying to keep alive will enrich the growth and lives of others. They form the soil and mulch that generate meaning from your mistakes.

Without nutrients in the ground of its formation, the seed cannot be planted. From one seed comes a vine. From the vine comes the fruit. From the fruit come even more seeds that give rise to even more plants. Just as Jesus was buried and from Him continue to come millions of new spiritual plants that bear marvelous grapes for making eternal wine, there are thousands of seeds that will come from you being planted. Transformation requires sacrifice, and I wonder if you have mislabeled the Husbandman's planting of you as Him condemning you to a graveyard. Far be it from the Eternal One to be so finite and temporary.

I encourage you to allow God's prison of purpose

in your life to do what it was intended to do: develop you into a strong vine. It's your location of cultivation. But when God escorts you out of your season of pain, be sure to leave behind the sorrow, bitterness, and anger, just like Nelson Mandela, who endured twenty-seven years in prison because he fought injustice. However, he said, "As I walked out the door toward the gate that would lead to my freedom, I knew if I didn't leave my bitterness and hatred behind, I'd still be in prison." After all, what good would it be for the Vinedresser to take you through the entire process only for you to give rise to mediocre fruit for sour wine? God isn't finished preparing you, yet. You are a seed designed to sprout. *Your fruit is becoming His wine.*

When you encounter trouble, what can you remind yourself about God's nature? How has God used trouble for your good in the past?

CHAPTER 5

Crushing Is Not the End

The reality is that we all suffer. We all suffer losing our children to gangs, to street drugs, to addictions we don't understand. We all suffer the indignities of aging and Alzheimer's, cancer and incarceration. We all suffer the economic roller coaster of less money and more bills. We all suffer the dislocation of our dreams and the explosion that Langston Hughes described so brilliantly when our dreams are deferred again and again and again.

We are all crushed by the same blows of life. But not everyone allows the crushing to destroy them.

Some discover the secret of making wine out of the remaining juice. They know how the blood of the vine becomes the fruit of the cup.

I visited my physician several weeks ago for my annual physical. While I was there, one of the attending nurses drew my blood to perform the customary screenings for diseases and other maladies. Medical professionals require a blood draw in order to see what they cannot see with the naked eye. Blood tells them just about everything they need to know in order to understand what is working and not working within the human body.

Similarly, experts in the justice system use blood analysis to determine vital information needed to solve crimes. Blood splatter analysts work in forensics departments and visit crime scenes to determine exactly what happened to a victim and the perpetrator by examining how and where the blood landed at the location. Similarly, law enforcement and forensics officers match blood from crime scenes with DNA on file to identify the guilty. And, conversely, blood collected years ago continues to exonerate individuals who were wrongfully incarcerated.

It appears, then, in addition to how the body uses and produces blood, that it acts as a testifying agent to actions others have not witnessed. Just like we notice in crimes, blood can act as a string that ties individuals to a certain act. No matter the time, each person involved in the crime is linked to the blood that was spilled. If we're able to determine who was present at a murder weeks, months, and even years later by blood testifying as to the identity of its owner, then blood becomes a witness to the past by its existence in the present.

If you compare the words *testify* and *testament*, they both have the same Latin root word, *testi*, literally meaning "witness." In the Bible we see this meaning tied to the emphasis God seems to place on the importance of blood. Time and time again, blood becomes a way to infuse life, to communicate, to reveal, to protect, to seal, to atone, and to save. For instance, in the Garden of Eden, when God sees that it is not good for man to be alone, the Lord creates woman from part of Adam's body. When Adam then states, "This is now bone of my bones and flesh of my flesh; she shall be called 'woman,' for she was taken out of man" (Gen. 2:23), he is speaking literally as well as figuratively.

The sons of Adam and Eve also discover the power of blood. Abel, having brought an acceptable sacrifice before the Lord, and Cain, offering one deemed unacceptable in God's sight, clashed as Cain's jealousy of his own brother led him to murder Abel. God's response to Cain is revealing: "The LORD said, 'What have you done? The voice of your brother's [innocent] blood is crying out to Me from the ground [for justice]'" (Gen. 4:10 AMP). The blood of the victim speaks, crying out for justice even after his life has ended.

In Exodus, when the people of Israel struggle to leave the slavery of Egypt behind, we see how the sprinkling of blood on Hebrew doorposts saved the inhabitants of the house from the wrath of the Angel of Death. The blood of slaughtered lambs shed on the altars in the temple became the means of atonement for people's sins prior to Christ's death on the cross. The contrast between these two is important because one was temporary—the bloodshed of animals for that moment's sacrifice—and the other eternal as

Jesus' shed blood and resurrection forever defeated sin and death.

Blood has amazing power. And Jesus reminds us that we cannot celebrate without it. In order to celebrate Jesus' resurrection, we have to first acknowledge the suffering and crushing of the cross. Jesus was crushed in every way—physically beaten, emotionally isolated, and spiritually bereft. Excruciating pain shot through every inch of His frame. Comfort was diabolically designed to be torturously beyond reach. As the nails in His hands became too much to bear, His body shifted His weight to His legs and feet, causing even more agony because of the nails in His ankles as well. Once the weight on His feet took its toll, Christ would pull Himself up by His nailed hands. With no way to escape the pain, He endured growing hypoxia that made each of His breaths more labored than the one before. His lack of blood was so severe that every one of His rapidly failing organs was starving for oxygen. In essence, Jesus was suffocating as a result of His extensive bodily trauma.

With a final heave of one last breath, Jesus gasped, *"It. Is. Finished!"*

The Darkness

The gospels of Matthew, Mark, and Luke bear witness to a darkness falling over Jerusalem at the time of Jesus' death, and that darkness remained for a span of three hours. Some have attempted to debunk the accounts of these three disciples by attributing that darkness to some natural phenomenon, like a solar eclipse or severe weather. Seeing as how I stand on the biblical account, taking nothing from it and adding nothing to it, I am led to believe that there was something else at play that led to the heavens giving no light at the time. Because the God who decided to express this recorded darkness is the same One who controls the weather and the rotation of the earth He created.

So why the darkness of those three hours? And why bring it to our attention?

I've had to comfort plenty of parents who have prematurely lost their children. I cannot and choose not to imagine an instance of giving the eulogy for my own sons or daughters and then burying them.

It's a nightmare I do not rehearse. Nevertheless, it is one that others have had the misfortune of suffering. I've seen their despair, heard their cries, attended the funerals, and had to counsel them through the resulting depression and suicidal thoughts. I say that to lay the groundwork for our understanding the emotional state of any parent who has lost a child. Perhaps you have. If so, you intimately know the pain associated with something so tragic.

If our emotions are given to us by our Creator, they must be modeled after His own emotions. After all, we know God laughs. He experiences joy, sorrow, and anger. The only difference between His emotions and ours that we can fully understand is that His are pure and haven't been corrupted by the stain of sin. With that being said, doesn't it stand to reason that He would experience His emotions on a level that far supersedes our own? So His sorrow at the sight of His Son dying and becoming the representation of evil that had so infected the human heart must have torn the Father apart. On top of that, the Father had to turn His back on the sin that Christ then embodied because righteousness and unrighteousness have no part with one another.

The Father forsook the Son He loved so that He could be reconnected back to us.

With the sorrow felt by the Almighty and His connection to every aspect of creation, I don't believe it's far-fetched that all of nature would react to the death of the glorious Son.

The darkening of the sun could be seen as a reflection of the Master weeping not only at what His Son became on our behalf, but also, I offer, at the fact that so few of His own people received him. The sun refusing to shine gave us tangible evidence that the light in God's eye had temporarily dimmed. Oh, yes. Surely, Jesus' sacrifice and resurrection would turn the world upside down and lead to the harvest of billions of souls throughout the rest of human history. But, at that moment, the Master, in His eternal nature, mourned the death of His beloved Boy.

Something else, however, was also happening at His death. Jesus gave up the ghost, meaning that His soul had departed His mortal body. Though His body would soon be placed in a tomb, His eternal spirit was already at work in the supernatural. Having reached backward and forward through time to grab hold of every sin humanity would commit, Jesus had taken upon Himself the punishment and death that we deserved. By entering the grave and conquering it on behalf of everyone who would receive Him—past, present, and future—Christ forced the grave to give up its first fruits of those saints who had gone on before as a testament to His work.

Only Matthew's recording of the gospel speaks to the breaking open of tombs and the appearance of dead saints walking around Jerusalem. I've seen many pastors and teachers overlook this fact out of fear of how to explain this phenomenon, but I hold to the notion that Jesus' presence in the grave on behalf of sin-stained humanity would not only force the grave to release a smattering of the faithful from its grasp but also upset earth itself.

After all, a new kind of man was being born—something that was the embodiment of the reconnection of God with his prized creation. In tandem with his sorrow, darkness fell and the foundations of the planet shook. Nevertheless, what if we looked at the accompanying earthquake as the heaving and pushing of a womb that was struggling to birth the newness placed in it by the seed of Jesus' sacrificial death?

Let's remember that Jesus suffered on our behalf and descended into the grave so that we might ascend back to our position of righteousness in God. He broke the shackles that bound us to sin and death. As a result, the grave had to release its hold on the faithful who lived before Christ arrived. Hence the earthquake. After He would ascend, so would they. The shaking of terra firma was not just a reaction to the Master's emotional tumult. No, it had to have been the pushing out of the first fruits of the new creation wrought by the planting of the seed of a sacrificial Savior. Just as a baby crowns when his head appears and approaches departure from the womb, so, too, did the first fruits emerge.

Without the crushing there would be no crowning! Suffering must never be wasted. Spilled blood is always redeemed. *Crushing is not the end.*

The Redemption

There are things in your life that you have placed in the ground because you have labeled them as dead. You have decreed that they don't have life and purpose. Perhaps you've walked away from a marriage or even bade farewell to your relationship with God. As your sorrow is still tangible, a thick darkness now surrounds your heart, and you are slow in returning to its gravesite because of the pain you once felt. That trauma caused a tremendous shaking in every aspect of your life, and you have taken an oath to never hope again, never dream again, never love again, and never again take a chance that life could be better.

But the very fact that life emerged from the grave as a response to Jesus' death suggests that what you've buried still has purpose. Yet, this truth is difficult for you to accept because you struggle to realize that its appearance is quite different from how you last saw it. Once corrupted with human effort and sin, it has returned wrapped in the glory of a Savior who wishes you would turn again and see the life that now inhabits it.

Whatever your passion may be—your dream, family, church, business, book—Jesus did not die just to save only you. His death was for every part of you that you had given up on. Look again. With the Master, it is being reborn as He steps out of His tomb with all power in His hands. Just like the resurrected saints that walked the streets of Jerusalem on the day of Jesus' death were the "crowning" of the birth that would come from His resurrection, that which you have buried is crowning.

Your crushing is nothing more than the beginning of a glorious transformation process that will reveal who and what you really are to the world and to you. And it's just the first step. Just like your acceptance of Jesus' death comes first, so does your crushing. Just like the grapes being trampled comes first, so does your crushing. There is more to come—so much more.

What have you given up on? Buried? How might it be redeemed in a new way, different than what you expect or what you experienced? What could be crowning now in your life?

CHAPTER 6

Make Some Wine

During our toughest and most challenging times, it can be hard to comprehend what God is up to. We may curse the pain and even doubt when we are in the midst of crushing, but as we grow and gain new insights, we can use the crushings of our past to remind us of God's faithfulness. It's the reminder that we have survived in the past and we will survive again.

Little did I know when I stood sweating in the Mississippi heat as a sixteen-year-old boy beside my father's grave that not only would I survive the devastating crushing of my soul, but I would also make new wine. Little could I imagine as I watched my car being repossessed that I would have more than enough wine for myself, my family, and others I'm allowed to bless. Little could I see how those sleepless nights would be more than worth the wine of meeting kings and presidents, ministering to millions of people around the world, and pastoring my flock.

My story is no different from what God is doing in your life. For everything you've lost, for all that's been trampled, let's make wine.

For every scar on your body and every fracture in your heart, let's make wine.

For every lost relationship and broken promise, let's make wine.

For every stolen dollar and wasted opportunity, let's make wine.

For every tear shed and every pain suffered, God is at work in your life.

Let's make wine!

Making wine requires more than changing the way you see your life. Spiritually speaking, making wine requires bloodshed. The importance of blood throughout Scripture cannot be overestimated because through it we see that our position with God is changed. As a result, it makes sense that our identities would change, as well. We see this transformative process illustrated in numerous ways throughout the Bible.

Look at Abram, who became Abraham. In establishing a new covenant with Abram, God's first order of business was changing Abram's identity. In Genesis 17:5, God moved Abram from one position to another by calling Abram to a different walk. Instead of pursuing his own path, Abram was to follow the path laid out for him by God, and that is precisely where many of us falter. We seek our own way, not understanding that our pride and arrogance lead us into destruction. We hate having to receive instructions from anyone because we think we have a handle on everything in our lives. As a result, we don't like relinquishing control and walking with God by faith.

We often make the mistake of labeling people based on what they've done. However, in labeling someone by what they've done, wouldn't we always be forced to call someone by what they did last? God doesn't do the same thing with us. The Master always calls us by what He has placed in us and what we will do for Him. I submit to you that God calls us what we will be while we're wrestling with what we were and what we did. When God changed Abram's name, He increased the distance between who the man once was and who God told him he would be in the future. To better understand that distance, all we must do is compare the names.

According to the text, *Abram* means "high/exalted father," while *Abraham* means "father of many nations." The covenant God initiated in Abram becoming Abraham points to something God has been doing with humanity for thousands of years. The Master continuously speaks the truth to mankind about who and what we are, and he confirms this new identity that we have through the shedding of blood. The sign of Abraham's new persona was that he was required to cut away the foreskin from his penis.

Other than the pain involved, this might seem insignificant until we take into account that the surrounding people in the land of Canaan didn't call for males to undergo the cutting until puberty or their entrance into marriage. Standing starkly in contrast to the people around him, Abraham was to not only circumcise every male in his house, but also to perform the rite on the eighth day of life. Eight being the number of new beginnings, each male entered into a new relationship with God on that day, being marked as someone else and part of something exclusive to everyone in his lineage.

Not only did Abraham receive a new name that signified who he was in God's eyes, but he and every man and boy in his house—indentured servants included—bore the physical proof that they were not like the men of the surrounding countries and societies. So exhaustive and complete was God's promise to Abraham that it not only extended to every man and boy associated with Abraham, but also to his wife, Sarai, who God renamed Sarah.

Through this point, you can see that God is not interested in just changing you and your life. He is complete, all-encompassing, consuming and filling everything and everyone that belongs to Him. God seeks not only your mind, or your heart, or your body. The Master wants the totality of who and what you are, because you will receive nothing less from

Him. As a result, Abraham could not be the only person that this new covenant would affect. Sarah had to be part of it because Sarah was one flesh with Abraham. God's blessings become reality in our lives when we rejoin the Master's plan by lining up with it in faith, like Abraham. In essence, when we reconnect with God, we step into what He has for us.

The Wait

A big part of becoming who God has called us to be looks like waiting to our human eyes. Yet, in the midst of our waiting, we are often being developed into the people God needs us to be for the next stage of our lives.

When I accepted my call into ministry, I remember pleading with God to allow me to preach. It was tough and often confusing. To be called and to sit in the background and listen to people speak from books of the Bible they couldn't even properly pronounce was the most aggravating experience of my life. It was during my inner court period that the Lord was developing my gift. I would be in the shower, preaching to bars of soap and washrags. I would be walking through the woods of West Virginia, laying hands on trees. All of this might sound comical to you, but I now see these moments as part of a season of fermentation, a critical part of the winemaking process. I spent years cleaning out the baptismal pool and leading devotional services before worship began, wondering when it would be my time to stand and proclaim the infallible Word of God. My heart would ache because I knew I had something to offer. Like the disciples, my heart was rent because the process didn't happen like I wanted.

But waiting was far more beneficial because the Lord was working on something marvelous in a secret place. He was working on my character. He was working on my heart. He was working on my nervousness. He was working on my motives. He was working on my wisdom. He was working on *me*, boiling off every single impurity because there was no way God was going to present to the world an unrefined, unfermented, underdeveloped product.

I was a minister for seven years before I preached

my first sermon, and I had hundreds of messages lined up and ready to go. But the Lord had me in a holding pattern, and it felt like it would never end. All of it was for a reason, and I didn't realize the greater reason—the wine reason—until Bishop Carlton Pearson called me to speak at Azusa. I preached a sermon there that was later seen by Paul Crouch. Paul Crouch saw only a piece of that sermon on television, but it was during a trying, pressing, and crushing time in his own life. It was just by God's handiwork and timing that Paul saw that one part of my sermon being played and, from there, called me and invited me to be on TBN.

During the fermentation period—the waiting time—you may be tempted to say there isn't much taking place, but you fail to realize that there is progress in the waiting. You may find yourself in a holding pattern but you don't realize that your flight has been moved from fortieth in line to second. This is because transition doesn't feel like work; it often feels like waiting. It feels like climbing a set of steps in a stairwell and finding yourself stuck as one foot hovers above the next step. You're in the position of being able to move up and forward but find that there's something else to be done before you are fully prepared to complete your climb. It's in that transitory moment of waiting that God is preparing you for the next step.

Just like in a holding pattern, the true work is hidden. A plane's pilot, not fully knowing what is happening on the ground, can only be patient while those in the air traffic control tower work out all the details. Otherwise, the plane might descend before the pilot has been given permission and slam into another jet that is taking off. Destruction comes swiftly on the heels of moving too soon. So, after crushing us, God exercises His grace by allowing us to ferment in the supposed stillness of transition so that we might be ready for the next stage.

Perhaps it's human nature, but I fear it only gets worse with each passing generation: we hate to wait. We've all been trained to get everything *now*. We have to buy now, move now, eat now, lead now, talk now, text now, enjoy now. We need the marriage now. We need the family now. We must have our company and business now. We want the fulfillment of our destinies *right now*, never minding the fact that God's grace is extended to us by allowing us to ferment in the holding pattern.

Although it may feel like it will never end, our fermentation is really just a brief time of transition. Life won't always be like this. Even in the face of the small amount of work that you can accomplish in the inner court after being crushed outside, the only thing the Vintner is requiring you to do is exercise patience. The ingredients are in place. You have been crushed and your juice extracted. Now it's time to let the divine process of transformation unfold.

The Simplicity of Winemaking

Winemaking basically comes down to three steps: crushing the grapes, allowing the juice to ferment, and collecting the wine. In other words, you mash the fruit, allow the juice to sit, and enjoy the results. That's it. Of course, there are other things that vintners have learned to do throughout history to refine and enhance their wines, but it takes little to no technology to create this beverage that humanity has enjoyed for thousands of years. The procedure is simple, direct, and to the point.

Particularly when it comes to fermentation, the process is rather straightforward. Fermentation is nothing more than the process in which the sugar in fruit is converted to alcohol because of its interaction with the natural yeast within its skins. After the grapes were crushed, a vintner in Jewish antiquity would allow the grapes and their juices to remain in their vats and ferment in the open air. As the yeast acted upon the sugar, it would produce a faint hissing sound similar to boiling. This resulted from the reaction in which carbon dioxide was released in the process. Apparently, some people who remained too close to the vats would be rendered unconscious. There are even reports of people being knocked out by the gases, then falling and drowning in fermenting wine.

Though fermentation is simple, the process is not to be disrespected. It still requires the vintner to keep a careful watch on the vats so that the wine does not turn to vinegar. You see, if too much time passes, the juice becomes bitter. Though some would allow the grapes to remain in the vats, other vintners would opt to place the fermenting juice in jars. Either way, the forthcoming wine was watched closely.

Carbon dioxide is a waste product expelled from organisms after a chemical reaction occurs. For instance, each time you exhale, you are releasing carbon dioxide. If you hold your breath for too long, you can pass out or suffocate because of the carbon dioxide buildup in your body, putting an abrupt end to something that should have continued to exist in another form. I suggest, then, that the fermentation process God takes us through acts as a spiritual broom He uses to sweep away what we no longer need. After all, in the midst of transformation, there must be a casting off of the old and an adherence to all that is new. One must give way to the other, for they cannot coexist.

Whatever it is the Master has placed on your heart to do for Him, I would suggest that He has taken, or will take, you through a season of hiding you. It's there that He gets you ready for your assignment. And you wouldn't be the first. Joseph was hidden in the pit and in prisons. Moses was hidden in the desert for forty years. David was hidden in the pastures while tending sheep. Jesus was hidden in Egypt as a child long before He endured His time in the tomb. Each of them was locked away and tended only by the Master Vintner, lest someone come along and disrupt their maturation process on the way to becoming wine.

I thank God for hiding me and releasing me when He was ready instead of when I was still fermenting. No matter how ready I thought I was to preach and move into the next level of my ministry, the Lord knew the time I needed to ferment and mature. His timing rarely seems to match our own impatience, but we must learn to release our haste in order to experience taste.

Too many of us rush to get to the end of the process, trying to tell God that we are ready for what He has for us when we've not even fully understood the gifts He has placed in us. We could be waiting and rehearsing when our time comes for the spotlight to shine on us as life's curtain goes up.

His timing may not reflect our expectations, but during fermentation we must practice patience and trust His perfect knowledge of the time required for us to reach maximum potency and flavor. The Master

Vintner knows when your wine is ready. He knows when your fermentation is done.

Reflect on your fermentation. What have you done during your waiting period? How has it served as a time to prepare you for what is next? How can you use your experience to help you during your next waiting period?

CHAPTER 7

Becoming

As we continue to explore the analogy of wine-making, I think it's important to remember what happens to the grapes right before they are crushed in the winemaking process. Just before the grapes are crushed, right when they are at their peak, blushed with ripe, juicy, sun-drenched flavor, filled with sweetness and nectar unlike any other, grapes become shells, remnants of their former uncrushed glory. Suddenly, there is no beauty about them at all.

And in those darkest moments we consider how—not if—we will ever be able to get back up and go on. We know ourselves only as empty husks of the ethereal dreams that once fueled our soul. But as we ferment and become wine, we must never forget that what we once were is nothing compared with what we are becoming.

I have never known anyone who is incredibly successful who did not have some dark, shameful, horrific place through which they had endured and suffered and agonized, filled with frightful anxiety that they might not survive. And then eventually, slowly and gradually, through tenacity and divine intervention and support from others, they, too, showed themselves to be alive.

They begin to feel their strength again. They realize they will never be the same, but what if they could go on? What if some diamond could emerge from the crushing weight applied to their soul? What if some priceless pearl could be extracted from the shell of who they once were?

When Jesus arose from the dead, it was the women who first saw the burial shroud crumpled like a sleeper's discarded blankets from the One who had awakened from death back into life. These women were the first, not because they were so filled with faith that they expected to find such a sight. No, they had come to their beloved Master's tomb out of loyalty, to decorate the stench with incense and myrrh.

But their loyalty and devotion intrigue me. They expressed no disappointment about placement, position, or politics. They refused to complain about their vulnerable investment in this spiritual venture that now seemed to mock them from the cross. No, these women remained loyal to what He used to be, not expecting anything else but to protect His image from passersby, to afford one last act of love and respect to Jesus of Nazareth.

Imagine their surprise and dismay and confusion when they found that there was no corpse, no body, no sign of Him. The grave had been disrupted. The stone had been rolled away. He was not there. What did this mean?

They carried the message back to the men. The first carriers of the gospel news were women. And it was not met with rejoicing, because who would believe something so fantastical? People can feel so low that others won't believe you can come out, so their news was met with disbelief and barely a skeptic's curiosity.

Peter and John ran down to see if it could be true or just another silly fabrication.

They entered, and…nothing! They backed up out of the grave, astonished at what they saw. He had risen. Not what they expected and yet, their minds must have gone into overdrive as they attempted to process this shocking, unthinkable turn of events. All the moments with their Master suddenly had to be revisited, reviewed, and recalibrated. Was this what Jesus meant all along?

Christ rose from the dead not only for each individual's salvation, but He also returned to bring resurrection power through the Holy Spirit to us collectively, as His body, His bride, the fellowship of believers known as the church. Most theologians and church historians consider Pentecost the turning point for the birth of the church. At Pentecost, believers gathered together for prayer and worship and received the gift of the Holy Spirit infusing their minds, their hearts, and their bodies with divine resurrection power.

And when we start talking about the glorious power of the Pentecost that birthed the church, we must realize that Pentecost sets its watch from the bloody, desolate place of the Passover. Pentecost was a place where the harvesters gathered to bring in the sheaves and reap the benefits of the toil of their labor. Only fifty days from the bloody tipping point of time and history, Pentecost revealed the gift emerging from God's most precious sacrifice.

Our weeping endures for a night, but joy comes in the morning. Whether we want to or not, all of us must pick up some kind of cross and follow Jesus into suffering. We all have our crosses to bear. A failed marriage, a special needs child, a debilitating injury, a chronic illness, unbearable debt. We all go through crushing, but we must never forget crushing is not the end. We go from the vineyard to the vat to the victory.

But clinging to that truth can be so hard when everything around you is slipping away. When I married my wife, I had a car, a good job, and a place to stay. But shortly after I said "I do," my car was totaled, my company had shut down, and I found myself struggling to buy food to feed our family. We used paper towels and duct tape to make diapers for our kids. We returned soda bottles and cans for change so we could buy groceries. I can remember stopping along the side of the road to pick up apples beneath a tree at the edge of the woods. I will never forget the nights I stared up at the sky and wondered if we would ever get beyond our struggles.

I'll never forget coming home from church one night and finding that Appalachian Power had turned off the power in our house. I couldn't bear to tell our kids, so young at the time, why we were in the dark, so instead I improvised on the spot and told them it was a game. I had turned off all the lights and whoever could get into bed without stubbing their toes would win. I didn't want my children to grow up poor and feel limited by that awareness. I wanted them to know it was possible to be people of color and have more than what I was able to show them at that time. I didn't know how, but I knew I had to endure beyond the crushing and trust there was life beyond this tomb.

A few years later, when I wrote my first book and my ministry was taking off, I bought a beautiful home with an indoor swimming pool, which was ironic because I couldn't swim. But I would pull up a chair and watch my kids splash and play, and it gave me the greatest joy to show them there was more. I wished my father could have lived long enough to witness such a sight and enjoy the wine now being opened from the crushing he had endured for my sake. He used to take our family for rides on Sunday afternoons, cruising through posh white neighborhoods to point out the houses that he cleaned during the week. He would describe the particular rugs and drapes of each one, the furniture and color of the rooms. Many of them often had the little black jockey statues near the driveway or in the manicured gardens.

I'm not the only one who struggles to see life beyond the tomb. I remember visiting Coretta Scott King once and admiring her plush apartment in Atlanta. When her house blew up decades before and the force of it knocked her back against the kitchen wall, she could not have known that one day she would be sharing the trauma as a story of survival from a luxurious home high above the city where her life was once endangered. But as her crushing fermented into the wine of experience, wisdom, and influence, she discovered a flavor she could not have anticipated at the time of her crushing.

Even after your pain has fermented and you find yourself in a new location, a new job, a new relationship, or a new lifestyle, you will still struggle. Like wine being poured from the vat into the bottles in order to be shipped and purchased and consumed, we must learn to be contained by new shapes. It's a part of the process.

Jesus said, "No one sews a patch of unshrunk cloth on an old garment, for the patch will pull away from the garment, making the tear worse. Neither do people pour new wine into old wineskins. If they do, the skins will burst; the wine will run out and the wineskins will be ruined. No, they pour new wine into new wineskins, and both are preserved" (Matt. 9:16–17).

The process of transformation for all of us begins with each of us. After we have endured our crushing, after some time has passed and we have experienced a different perspective that ferments our pain into personal power, we must then begin our life as new wine. We must accept that nothing will ever be the same again. We cannot reclaim, repair, or recycle that which has been lost or broken. We must begin again knowing that we have new wine to offer. Like Lazarus returned to life and leaving the tomb, we must unwrap the burial cloths from our bodies.

It's time to stop living in the past. It's time to leave your tomb behind. It's time to taste the new wine God is producing in your life.

Write a journal entry celebrating your transformation. What are you leaving behind? What are you looking forward to as a part of your new life?

CHAPTER 8

God Is with You

I had an amazing opportunity to visit the Western Wall, the only remaining structure of what used to be Herod's temple in Jerusalem. The Wailing Wall stands over sixty feet high and is sixteen hundred feet long. The entire area was filled with tourists taking pictures and observing the holiest site in Judaism.

I noticed something that piqued my curiosity. Many people were writing their prayers on paper and slipping them into the cracks of the wall. I, too, joined in this exercise and placed my written prayer in the wall. But, as I stepped away, I noticed the Orthodox Jews who visited the wall placed their prayers in a fissure. However, they moved their bodies in a certain way. As they prayed, each of them rocked back and forth, continuously moving. My keen guide noticed me looking at the Jews moving and quickly filled me in. He said, "They rock as an homage to how God moved with them in the wilderness. Wherever the people of Israel went, Yahweh went with them."

In a few moments, within my own mind and heart, I had a powerful sermon about this ritual already prepared. God, the Almighty Creator of the universe, traveled *with* Israel. He lived and moved among His children in the midst of the wilderness, guiding them in their wandering. What intrigues me most about the Lord's characteristics is His willingness to not only move *with* His people, but His penchant for relocating His chosen ones before He puts His plan into effect.

Can you see why this matters? *God's hand and presence are standing front and center in any and every stage of our crushing.* To not see He who has promised to never leave you or forsake you during your days of calamity is enough to cause you to abandon hope that life will get any better. So if we see the Orthodox Jews in constant motion while in the midst of their prayers to pay respect to the fact that God was moving with Israel in the wilderness, don't their actions beg us to pay attention? Shouldn't we look for God's presence in our own movements and transitions in life? And if we look for Him, how can we find Him?

One of the ways to answer this question, I believe, requires that we consider what it means to spend time with God, to get to know Him and to communicate with Him. Though time given to our numerous responsibilities requires our full attention, I quickly learned as an adult that I also need to set aside time for myself and my family. To give all of yourself to everyone and everything else and leave little, if any, of you to your family and yourself is to do your future and your destiny a grave disservice. There is something to be said for the value of being alone and taking a break from it all. It makes no sense to arrive at the fruition of your destiny and have little to no strength to walk in it.

Everyone must learn the value, healing qualities,

and even necessity of being alone to rest, recharge, receive divine insight, and purge what has been affecting them. Always being surrounded by people and standing in the presence of others prevents one from experiencing the blessings found only in solitude.

You must make time for rest a priority. Even more to the point, you must discover that certain blessings and assets are found only in rest. Better still, some advantages emerge exclusively in and while being alone. I think my best thoughts when I'm alone, and I move faster without the weight of other responsibilities and distractions. Plus, the Father loves to speak, especially when there are no distractions between the two of us.

The Husbandman recognizes the value of seclusion because He values the harvest and wine His fruit will produce. I have noticed that He has the propensity to remove and relocate individuals chosen to complete tasks for His Kingdom from among crowds or familiar environments. It is rare to see God calling someone to a unique destiny and allowing them to remain where they've always been. I'm hard-pressed to think of a single instance. It's almost as if He wishes to cultivate something within them.

We see this pattern throughout Scripture. Noah, the first vintner, experienced his own loneliness when he was called away to build the Ark. Abraham was told to leave the land of his fathers for a place that God would show him before He brought Abraham into covenant with Him. Joseph was sold into slavery by his own brothers and, while he was away from his family, God trained him to run Egypt. Moses, after having become a murderer, was driven to the wilderness, where he meets God and receives His orders to be the voice and deliverer to free the children of Israel. David, considered to be the runt of his family, was alone during his on-the-job training that prepared him to be Saul's successor as the king of Israel. The gospels are replete with instances of Jesus withdrawing to be alone and pray.

To the untrained eye, all of this would seem like wandering and meandering without a purpose. Could there be more to it, though?

We see that being alone for a season is valuable in God's sight, but I don't want you to harp on the aloneness we have previously discussed. I'm calling your attention to God's penchant to move you into the position and place that is most strategic for His will while you experience a feeling of being lost. He doesn't do this just to prepare you. He does this because the first thing we see God doing when we initially meet Him in the first chapter of Genesis is hovering, brooding, breathing, and moving over the darkness and void that existed before He called the wandering, formless, nothingness to order and commanded light to explode onto the scene.

So what does this tell us?

Quite simply, we do not serve a stagnant, motionless, dormant, inactive, or idle God. From the first time we meet Him, we see that God is always on the move. God's movement suggests progress and purpose. And though He may be silent during certain seasons, we must accept the fact that our God is a perpetually moving God. Now, if we see that God is always moving with purpose, who are we to think that we would be different from the Master who created us? God will move us to accomplish His ultimate goal and purpose in and for our lives.

Time with God

If you're looking around at the various aspects of your life and see ubiquitous isolation or seclusion, know that you are being groomed for something special, and the Master wants to interfere in the process. Unfortunately, detachment often carries with it a certain degree of pain because each of us, on some level, requires interaction with another human being. After all, even the Master says it's not good for man to be permanently alone. Thankfully, in those moments when we are by ourselves, God's habit of communicating with us shows itself.

I've already shared some of my personal instances of being up at night, trying to wrap my head around challenging circumstances. But in addition to thinking, feeling, and grieving over the situations that resulted in my restless, sleepless night, I also experienced something else. After getting tired of pacing, I would quiet myself and listen out for God's still, small voice of direction or correction.

God never failed to speak to me. Oh, He might

have waited to do so, but He has never stopped communicating with me. Rather, I discovered that I had to allow God to be God and communicate with me in the manner He thought best for the moment. After silencing the loud angst of my mind, I would hear Him speak words of peace to my troubled soul and provide steps that, once executed, would cause me to wonder why I had worried so much in the first place. I'm telling you that there is something about God's presence and His ability to impart wisdom, identity, and peace in those times of uncertainty.

It's like going on a date. When was the last time you went out on a date? I'm not talking about simply meeting up with someone new. I speak of going all out and setting the stage for an experience with and for the one you love—creating a moment they will never forget. I don't ask in order to foster feelings of embarrassment for those who haven't dated in some time, and neither am I asking to further vaunt feelings of accomplishment for those who have. My question highlights the reason behind dating.

Though our contemporary society has changed what it means to date someone, the impetus behind dating and courting an individual is to woo them. When viewed in that light, the wooer calls out the one he or she is pursuing, the one he or she wants to love, and to whom he or she wishes to show him- or herself. Remember the value we discovered in being alone and how the Master delivered Israel out of the hands of its oppressor? From there, Israel goes directly to the wilderness, and God's design for them was that they worship Him and come into relationship with Him. God did this with His mighty arm, and showed even more of Himself to them.

He fed them bread and quail directly from His table while giving them water from His rock, effectively treating His people to a five-star dinner. All of this happened as He cooled Israel during the day with His cloud that guided them and His romantic fire that warmed them at night. God *courted* Israel in the wilderness, showing them a scant measure of His capabilities in loving them every day. And, when He wanted to be close to them, God gave them the specifications of the setting in which He would meet them: El Moed, the tent of meeting, or Moses' tabernacle.

The tent of meeting was portable and would move

with the entire camp. There, sacrifices would be offered up by the priests on a daily basis, and the high priest would enter the most holy place of the tent once a year on Israel's behalf.

Understand, though, the forty years of Israel's wandering in the wilderness was more than a form of punishment for their unbelief in their Deliverer-God, which Scripture points out (Num. 14:34). Yes, Israel's unbelief doomed them to wander a year for every day they were allowed to examine the vastness and beauty of the blessed Promised Land God had sworn to give them. But consider what led God to call Abraham His friend—the fact that Abraham believed God. If Abraham's belief in God caused God to want to enter into a covenant relationship with Him, then Israel's wandering in the wilderness because of their unbelief wasn't something God issued simply because He likes torturing people. Proverbs reminds us of a greater motive: "For whom the LORD loves He corrects, Even as a father *corrects* the son in whom He delights" (Prov. 3:12 AMP).

And just as God did with Israel, He is calling you out of the land of your oppression, your addiction, your pain, and the circumstances that have you believing that you will never get back up again. He has opened the door for you to begin your exodus, but you must put every ounce of your faith and trust in Him to do only what He can do, which is take care of you. He is calling you out so that you might worship Him and so that He might be given the opportunity to develop a relationship with you outside the purview of your abusers and your deadly habits. And, though He has called you to be with Him in the wilderness and witness how much He loves you, I will not ignore the overwhelming feeling that many experience when they are freed from any oppression.

They experience the sensation of being disoriented in the midst of their straggling.

We wander because we long for the days of familiarity, even when those days brought horrendous moments of pain, anguish, and a complete lack of hope. Because the first thing a person does when they are brought into a new space is to begin seeking out a way to stabilize themselves in the unfamiliar. Seeing that they can find no recognizable handle to hold on to in a new season, they look backward to something commonplace in order to receive comfort. For many, their comfort is pornography, even when it caused the end of their marriage. For others, it's alcohol abuse, though their liver is so hard and kidneys so shriveled that they've found themselves on a transplant list. For some, it's the warmth of the arms of a previous lover, even though the hands attached to those arms have left marks and bruises on their faces that have forced them to lie in order to explain away their existence.

You would be surprised at what people do just to put themselves at ease during their season of wandering—that season when you look to something else in place of the God that freed you because even your Deliverer looks so strange to you that you would opt for destruction. After all, you're unable to tell the difference between the safe harbor of His presence and the rocky shores of destitution. The coping mechanisms you've employed during your wandering have caused you to become spatially disoriented.

Like we see in the lives of the children of Israel and those who have suffered at the hands of abusers, could it be that our real problem of unbelief stems from the reality that we have put more of our faith in what and who has traumatized us than we have in the God who loves us? Is it possible, then, that our wandering because of our disbelief in the truth of God is a tool the Master uses to get "Egypt" out of us?

What if the final stage of the crushing process is meant to ensure an eternal cohabitation between God and His people, both of them being forever reconnected? What if having God inside us is the agent of spiritual fermentation needed to transform us into wine?

Answer the questions asked in this chapter and reflect on how time with God can help you transform.

CHAPTER 9

The Pairing

Wine pairing brings out a new dimension to the taste of wines. In wine pairing, you learn that red wines pair best with bolder-flavored red meats and savory dishes, while white wines go well with fish, seafood, and chicken. You want a wine that complements and even enhances the food while possessing its own intensity and flavor.

While wine pairing is enjoyable and gives you a new appreciation for fine dining, there is another pairing that yields even more benefits. It's the relationship between you and the Master. Your relationship with God exhausts the length of all time because an eternal God cannot produce anything less than an eternal seed. Therefore, each of us is intended for the ever after. We are eternal spirits temporarily in earthly bodies.

You and God have been locked into a timeless relationship that only paused when you were born into the earth. Eternity past and eternity future are separated only by the slender sliver of time in which you and I now exist in this lifetime on earth. Before time began, you were with God, and when time ends, you will be with Him again. Simply put, you and God were meant for each other.

No matter how hard you might try, you can't escape the spiritual bond between you and your Maker. You can't drink it away. You can't smoke it away. You can't sex it away. You can attempt to walk away from God and live your life as you see fit, but the Master has placed a hook in you that prevents you from doing anything that would spoil the future wine He is laboring to produce in you. In other words, He remains faithful even when we don't. Despite our attempts to escape our crushing, God is intent on converting us from one level of life to another one.

What He is doing with you is not built on your finished work. Your salvation and new identity are built on the finished work of Christ, and that finished work was done with everlasting effect just as He is God forever. As we have seen, we can look throughout all the Old Testament until now and see the Master's blood-red wine seeping out of eternity and into this present moment.

God has promised that we will find Him if we seek Him (Jer. 29:13). From all my years of actively pursuing God, though, I've discovered that He loves to play hide-and-seek. He doesn't always hide in the most obvious places, but He leaves a trail of spiritual bread crumbs for us to follow when He's chosen an out-of-the-way place in which to conceal Himself. God is easily spotted during our joyous seasons, but it often seems as if he's an expert at tucking Himself away in the most obscure locations during our trying times.

Could it be, however, that God hasn't hidden Himself during our tumultuous seasons, but rather He has simply revealed Himself in a form we've yet to recognize? After all, even the disciples at first believed Jesus was a ghost when they saw Him walking on the wind-tossed sea. No wonder, then, that they demanded to see Him for themselves after He arose from the tomb. They couldn't grasp how Christ could so dramatically change the course of nature as they understood it and still be the Master they knew and loved.

Before we criticize their reluctance to recognize Him, we might look first at our own ability to spot God in our lives. Tell me, can you recognize God in another form, or must He always reveal Himself to you through the construct of your familiarity?

The Vinedresser wouldn't have gone to all of the trouble to develop us if He was going to destroy us. If the Lord wanted us dead, He could have killed us before we ever brought forth fruit.

Refinement

Have you ever desired something for so long that you resolved in yourself that it was never going to happen? Have you ever had to declare that your dreams were dead so that you would finally have a moment's peace? It's the delay in the fulfillment of the promises of God that causes us so much pain. When the Master gives us the vision of what He's going to do in our lives, He shows us the mountain peaks while He hides the valleys. If you saw the climb you would have to endure to get to the mountaintop, you would abandon the entire trip.

It's the passion we have for the fulfillment of God's promise that drives us, but it's the play between the pain and passion that He uses to refine us. It's our passions we have to make peace with when we are confronted with the delayed realization of God's promises because passion makes you dissatisfied with what you have as you wait for what you want. In the face of waiting to be paired again with God, we fight with putting our hopes to bed in order that we might deal with the agony of delay. So we cry our dreams to sleep because it's easier for us to allow our passions to rest instead of allowing them to remain and go unfulfilled.

But the Master is not in the business of torturing His children through delays. Rather, it's the hidden things in the valleys of "not yet" and "wait" that make us who we are. God gets our attention with the hidden things that lie in wait in the valleys—the things that happen that we didn't see coming or expect.

It's the problems that catch us off guard that are so alarming and amazing. During those times you have to decide how you're going to react to what happens to you because you can't control what life throws your way. But you do have a choice in how you will respond. Do you give up on God, put your dreams to the side, and make up in your mind that the promises of God will never come to pass?

Or do you trust the One that holds you even though the valleys of life threaten to claim your faith as their next casualty? If God uses our valleys to prepare us for the peaks, we must realize that we are not yet ready for the promises that reside at such a great height. After all, God hides His treasures until we can handle them. And since we can't see the value of what's coming, we don't look for the incredible. It's while we're not looking that things are moving. It's while we're sleeping in the valleys that God does His best work because the Master does not need our help as He transforms us. He requires only our faith and humility.

I am thoroughly convinced that God made me who I am in the low places of my life. It's the nights I cried myself to sleep and my tears crawled across the bridge of my nose that God most often used to develop me into the person I am today. It was the hidden things in the valleys that God used to kill off my fleshly desires and strip from me everything that would prevent me from being His wine. I had to learn not to fear my valley experiences but accept them—and that process continues. And I believe you must do the same.

We know God's going to do something, but we don't know when. We know God is going to bless us, but we don't know how. We know God is going to connect us, but we don't know through whom. God told you He was going to deliver you, but He didn't tell you what He was going to deliver you from. God said you'd be together with Him again, but He didn't tell you everything you'd endure along the way. All of this is preparation for your final pairing with the Master. You're doing everything to avoid the hidden crushings in the valleys, but those are needed to bring you to the point of being reunited and paired with God. Don't get lost by the distractions.

Just as Jesus experienced the turmoil, pain, and depression in the low parts of His life before His transformation, we will experience the same. If we were meant to reunite with Him in eternity, we must make the same journey through the valleys of preparation that He did. You didn't simply tumble into trauma. You were led into it, escorted into it by the Master Vintner who so wants to be with you that He said, "Look. I'll go first. I'll endure the crushing to become wine."

The blessings and transformation we've sought for so long have been promised to us by a God who did not free us from bondage just to be destroyed in the deserts and valleys of unbelief and unfulfilled longings. Do not retreat back to the familiar caves of abandoned hopes and deceased dreams. The eternal pairing we once enjoyed with the Father is coming in short order. And though you may be crying, "Don't make me hope again," the Master is showing Himself to you in a different and newer form that is proof that none of what you experienced is in vain. Even your delays are fitting into His plan to prepare you.

The new form God has taken is the one you will

one day assume for your pairing when you and He are finally together for all eternity. Your wine will last for all of time. Don't sacrifice the quality because you can't see beyond your pain. Trust Him. He knows exactly—*exactly*—what it's like to endure the crushing you've been through. God is committed to you through it all and beyond. Your pairing with Him knows no end.

How does it make you feel to know that God wants an eternal pairing with you? Spend time with God, thanking Him for the gift of eternal pairing. Recommit to trust in Him no matter what you are going through or where you find yourself wandering.

CHAPTER 10

Pressing On

The beauty of every ounce of wine we carry is contained by what our Lord Jesus did for us in the Most Holy Place. He was, in fact, the first to RSVP to God's eternal invitation:

> But when Christ appeared as a high priest of the
> good things that have come, then through the
> greater and more perfect tent (not made with
> hands, that is, not of this creation) he entered once
> for all into the holy places, not by means of the
> blood of goats and calves but by means of His own
> blood, thus securing an eternal redemption. For if

the blood of goats and bulls, and the sprinkling of
defiled persons with the ashes of a heifer, sanctify
for the purification of the flesh, how much more
will the blood of Christ, who through the eternal
Spirit offered Himself without blemish to God,
purify our conscience from dead works to serve the
living God. (Heb. 9:11–14 ESV)

Jesus did not arrive at the mercy seat through the
temporary blood of animals. All at once, Jesus was
both the sacrifice that was crushed and our High
Priest. Therefore, the blood He sprinkled upon the
mercy seat in the eternal tabernacle was His own and
a foretaste of what we would become after He trans-
formed us. In essence, Jesus brought His own wine to
the intimate tasting at God's table.

And seeing that what the Vintner does in our lives
is patterned directly after what happened in Christ's
resurrection, the Vintner calls us to the secret cham-
bers of His presence, too. It's with the Master that we
finally see something we've not seen in the previous
compartments of the tabernacle. We see that there

is no more crushing, no more refinement or process, and no more struggle and strife. Instead, the process has been replaced by something altogether different. Instead of work, there is only relationship and being who we truly are—the wine of our King.

When it comes to what God has done in our lives, the transformation through which He has taken us, and what we are called to, it is important that we remove from our minds the stages of old. There is nothing wrong with remembering how the Father has carried you. However, we often have a penchant for clinging to the past at the expense of our futures. Now that we are wine, we cannot afford to continue thinking like grapes, remaining in the outer court and not pressing on to greater things.

As a result, the wine is brought to the last compartment of the tabernacle—the Most Holy Place. Here we step into the temple befitting the joy of God's final harvest festival. Here in this Most Holy Place the Vintner invites us to a private communion with Him so that we might sample together what He has created in us along with His plans to share us with the world.

In this festival, it's not only a reuniting of our Father with His children, but also a modern coming together of the wine and bread in a celestial upper room experience reminiscent of what Jesus did in that Last Supper with His disciples. This is a holy house party like no other. It all comes full circle now: the symbolic parts and sacred pieces of the tabernacle in the Old Testament; the reality of the Incarnation as Jesus became human in order to suffer for our sins, die on the cross, and rise again; and the crushing you have experienced in your own life in order to become the precious, holy wine fit for a King.

This eternal nature we carry within us directs us to the day when we will no longer need physical sustenance but will subsist only on the spiritual bread that Christ gave to His disciples in the upper room in the form of physical bread. If you remember, however, bread wasn't the only thing Jesus offered them. With that bread, He gave them wine, a symbol of the blood that was spilled on our behalf and placed on the mercy seat.

Through the crushing brokenness Christ endured, His blood became the new wine after which our transformation was patterned. We were destined to become that same kind of wine by the same Vintner and His process of crushing us. In essence, then, the bread of life and wine of the spirit have beckoned us with glad hearts into God's presence so that we would enjoy a higher, better, and eternal communion with Him.

Only in this new communion, we find one special difference. Now there is intimacy, a give and a take between one another. Where the Master would give, we would receive. Now that we are like Him as His wine, we offer ourselves to Him so that He would delight in what we have become. There is no need for us to be bread, because His body serves as that for us.

Like the most excellent host, God supplied for us what we could not supply for ourselves. And because His supply is never depleted, we needn't worry about this feast ending soon. Seeing that the wine we embody is eternal and connected directly to Him, we, too, will never run dry. Therefore, this festival will never end, but continue unhindered between the Master Vintner and His new cask of wine—His new creation.

A New Creation

As we embrace being God's new creation in Christ, as we grow accustomed to living as His holy wine, then we begin experiencing new levels of joy, peace, contentment, purpose, and satisfaction. No longer do we wonder why we are here on this earth. We know that everything we have been through is more than worth it because God has used it all, wasting nothing, to bring us to the point in our lives where we are now.

Your crushing is not the end—it's only the beginning. It is where you are planted for purpose—God's purpose. One's crushing always gives rise to something wonderful in someone else's life. Jesus was the first example and we now follow His example.

I'm far from perfect, but I have experienced the blessing of being holy wine to those around me. And lest you think I boast, please understand that what I'm called to do humbles me on a daily basis. There is no way I can do anything on my own. But through Christ, I can do all things.

Jesus took for us what we would never be able to

handle on our own, but the Master was not content with just saving us. No! He wishes for us to be like Him so that we would be intimate and commune with Him. And, though He bore the punishment for all our transgressions and sin, He endeavored to take us through the process of preparing us for the face-to-face meeting we would have with the Father.

Hence, our crushing. Hence, our planting or replanting.

Having survived and thrived in the crushing and fermentation, though, we can now hear the heavy locks of the eternal doors to His presence release, because on the other side of the thick veil stands the Almighty God who wishes an audience with us even more than we do with Him. For during the conversation we would have with Him, our Father desires to partake of a vintage He has on His Son's authority is "a very good year"!

You may struggle to see yourself as God's holy wine now, and that's understandable. But the truth of the matter is that you are not what and who you used to be. You are not what you did. You are not your lack. You are not what people have labeled you to be, and God will continue confronting you to make you understand who you are.

You are not a grape. You are not even the crushed hull and flesh that remains after being trampled. You are something far better. You are wine. When God sees you, He sees you as perfect. When God's eyes rest on you, He doesn't see who and what you used to be; instead, He sees the fully developed you in Christ. He sees the righteous you. In the Bible we're told that we are the righteousness of God in Christ (2 Cor. 5:21) and that in this world we are as He is (1 John 4:17). God's Word tells the truth about who you are—so believe it!

I realize it can be challenging to accept the truth about who you are. If the Bible has been telling people the truth about themselves for thousands of years, you would think that people would have gotten the message by now. That would be the logical conclusion, but you would be completely taken aback by how arduous it is to get people to simply walk in what they believe. Just think about it. The ramifications of walking in the faith we profess are immense.

Do you understand that Jesus has already done everything for you?

You must accept this truth because God is more than satisfied with the wine He has produced in you. He is elated with how you have turned out, keeping a cask unto Himself as a trophy proudly displayed in His personal winery. But He has a plan for the rest of your bottled vintage that entails you being offered to the world as a sign for what He wants to do with other grapes.

The Vintner wants others to taste the masterpiece He has produced in His new creation. You have His power within you. You have full access to all the riches in Christ. He wants you to offer hope to those being crushed and struggling to understand. He wants to work through you to comfort the desolate, heal the sick, strengthen the weak, and reveal the light of His love in a dim world.

You are God's trophy, and He wants to show you off.

Remember, God has designed, equipped, and called each of us to accomplish many great things. He has given us a vision, promising that He would bring it to pass. Why, then, are we so prone to lose sight of the fact that the Master is the one who gave us the idea and not the other way around? Probably more than anything else, the one message I have to tell people that I mentor and counsel over and over and over again is that God's timing is flawless. His clock is perfect.

Over and over again, I have to thank God for sticking with his timetable for my life and not bending to my will. I can look back over my life and see where God could have answered me right then with what I thought I wanted and allowed it to destroy me. With the utmost gratitude, I salute Him for keeping from me what I considered the best thing for me at the time.

If you're anything like me, you realize the folly of begging God for something, and when He gives it to you, you murmur and complain about what you got. We have the craziest habit of wanting what we want until we get it. Whereas if we waited for the fullness of God's timing to come to pass, we would see that His ordained season carries within it an unforeseen amount of grace and protection.

We must remember that our God sees the end from the beginning. There is no problem for which He doesn't already have a solution.

Everything God does is strategic. Never do we witness God making a mistake or running late for His divine appointments with us. Though I might be taken by surprise with the situations that befall me in life, there has never been a moment when I ran to God with the words "Lord, I didn't even see this coming" and He responded, "I didn't either!"

Throughout this entire book, we've been discussing how the Lord develops and transforms us. Across these pages, you've repeatedly read the word *process*. This word, in and of itself, denotes the passage of time. For the most part, transformation isn't an event, and it's definitely not something that happens only once. As I continue to grow in my relationship with the Lord, I am appreciating the fact that He takes His time with me. He doesn't rush with any of us because anything valuable is also something worth waiting for. After all, excellence is not produced in haste.

But there are occasions when it seems like there is no time for process—those moments when something must be done *now*. There is no waiting. There are no seasons. There comes a time in your life when you need a word, a solution, or a miracle now. When dying on the operating table, you don't need someone to run you through the process of the entire surgery. The surgeon should have started working the day before!

We see this with the woman with the issue of blood. The woman was already dying, and we infer that it was her desperation for healing that drove her to press through the crowd and touch the hem of Jesus' garment. Or what of the woman who was bent and bowed over for eighteen years (Luke 13:12)? Was it better for the Lord to tell her about what He would do to heal her or say, "Woman, thou art loosed"?

What I am trying to get you to see is that, though the Lord develops us through a process that transforms us, He is fully aware of those moments when a season of change will take too long. There are times in our lives when He instantly brings forth in us what is necessary at that moment. Those are the instances when He moves from working on us through process to making us immediately incredible.

God's Best

During the process of our crushing, fermentation, and transformation into God's wine, we often lose sight of what our Master is doing and become consumed with impatience. "When, Lord?" we ask. "When will I see what you're up to? When will my pain stop? When will my life turn around? When will my loss subside? When will I experience your joy and peace? *When, Lord, when?*"

Perhaps you're asking that question right now. You've sensed that the Vintner has been doing a mighty work in your life and that He has bottled you for distribution or is ready to pour you out for all the world to taste. However, there seems to be a delay, and you're questioning Him about when He will do what He said He was going to do. You see others experiencing and walking in their promise while wondering when your day will come.

But remember, God always saves the best for last.

Do you realize that what took some people fifteen or even twenty years to accomplish, God can bring about for you in less than a day? So when it comes to the question of "when" that burns in your heart, remember that the same Husbandman who matured and cultivated you in your vine and grape stages is the same Vintner who crushed, fermented, and bottled you in your wine stages.

God is fully aware of your times and seasons. You needn't worry about anything, save keeping your eyes on the Master who has already called over the servants who will present what you have to the supervisor of the feast. The party is in full swing. The guests are present. Man's temporary and less-desirable wine is running out, like it did at the wedding where Jesus performed his first miracle (see John 2:1–12). Your time is almost here. Remain patient. Your water is about to be drawn out to be sampled and served.

Crushing is never the end.

Your best is yet to come! You will bloom yet again.

Thank God for the seasons you've experienced throughout life. Think about where you are now and what God could be preparing you for or protecting you from. Determine to stick with God throughout your seasons, knowing this is not your end and you will bloom within your purpose and God's intended season.

About the Author

T. D. JAKES is the #1 *New York Times* best-selling author of more than forty books and is the CEO of TDJ Enterprises, LLP. His television ministry program, *The Potter's Touch*, is watched by 3.3 million viewers every week. He has produced Grammy Award–winning music as well as hit films such as *Heaven Is for Real*, *Miracles from Heaven*, and *Jumping the Broom*. A master communicator, he hosts MegaFest, Woman Thou Art Loosed, and other conferences attended by tens of thousands. He lives in Dallas, Texas.